MW01066008

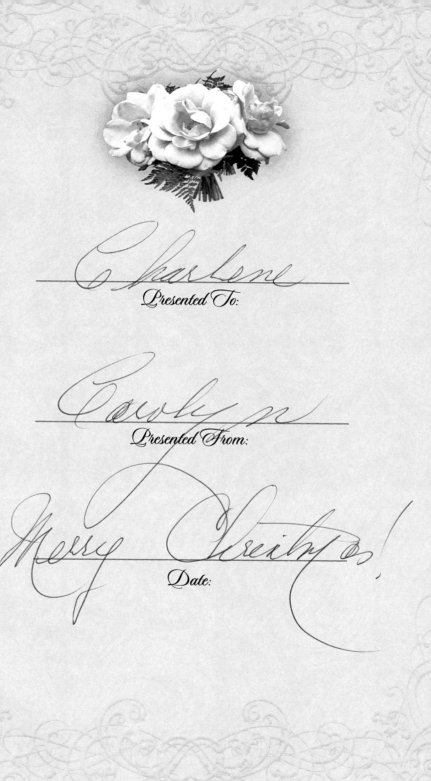

_Charlene_

Presented To:

_Carolyn_

Presented From:

_Merry Christmas!_

Date:

# Wisdom Mama's Way

*An Inspirational Scriptural Guide To Life*

## CAROLYN A. ZALOGA

*Wisdom Mama's Way*
ISBN 978-0-615-17591-1
Copyright © 2007 by Carolyn Zaloga

Library of Congress Control Number: 2007909448


Published by
Victory Graphics and Media
9731 East 54th Street
Tulsa, OK 74146
www.victorygraphicsandmedia.com

# Contents

## Introduction

Mama was a friend whom I met in my youth. Through the years it became obvious that she had a lot of wisdom. I was impressed to the point of taking notes. This book is the result of those notes.

Mama had a unique style of self-expression. Her words were simple, to the point and easily understood. I have tried to reflect her style by quoting her directly in many instances.

She is now in heaven with the Lord. I hope you get as much joy and pleasure from her words as I did when I was listening.

This book is a memorial to her counseling and guidance through many years of my life.

Whenever I am asked whether she was really my mother, I respond with, "She was my mother in Jesus."

## The Four of You

Always remember that whatever your problem, the four of you can handle anything. You have you. You have God the Father. You have God the Son Jesus. You have God the Holy Spirit. The four of you can handle anything.

Wear the world as a loose garment; but take Jesus as your friend. We human beings are incredibly precious to God. He spends most of His time on us. He is involved in everything. If God said it in His Word, agree with Him. Your arms are too short to box with God.

He will work it out for you. He will make a way wherein there is no way. Let Him work it out for you. There is no problem too big for God. Nobody can do you like Jesus!

*"...for without me*

*ye can do nothing."*

John 15:5

## Life's Secret

Life's secret to victory is prayer, prayer! God hears all of it—just you and God. That way He can quiet your mind and heart. Being still before Him allows the Lord to saturate you with calmness and His peace.

Your daily troubles get the chance to diminish in comparison to His strength. God is concerned about you. The devil deceives us into thinking we really don't need to pray and shouldn't take the time to pray and wait upon God; but he's on death row. Don't even think about him. Don't give him any shelf space. Seek the gift of faith in prayer. Expect results. Believe that God is telling you the truth. You can't make it without Jesus, so don't even try.

God promises to hear us and answer.

"Therefore I will look unto the LORD;
I will wait for the God of my salvation:
my God will hear me."

Micah 7:7

"Call unto me, and I will answer thee,
and show thee great and mighty things,
which thou knowest not."

Jeremiah 33:3

"It is good that a man should both hope and
quietly wait for the salvation of the LORD."

Lamentations 3:26

## Faith

If you're going to have faith in God—have it!

In the storms of life, Jesus will walk with you, direct you, comfort you, guide you, nourish your heart and encourage you when your faith is weak. He is on your team. He wants you to be happy and satisfied in Him.

The music we listen to, the literature we read and the company we keep affect us. Read biographies of faithful Christians. Where is your faith? Is it still in yourself?

God is your source. Don't put your faith and trust in man because he is weak. See in the Spirit. We walk by faith, not by sight. We get impatient. Why does it take so long?

God will answer your petition, maybe not on your time, but He's never too late. You don't have to be rich to have faith in God. Your outcome in life depends on how much confidence you have in God to see you through. God takes us through one test at a time. Each one just a little bit further in faith. Collapse in His strong arms through just one more test. He will take you the rest of the way.

Don't worry. He is able to hold you.

"He shall not be afraid of evil tidings:
his heart is fixed, trusting in the LORD."

Psalm 112:7

"Cast not away therefore your confidence,
which hath great recompence of reward."

Hebrews 10:35

"But without faith it is impossible to please him:
for he that cometh to God must believe
that he is, and that he is a rewarder
of them that diligently seek him."

Hebrews 11:6

"That the trial of your faith, being much
more precious than of gold that perisheth,
though it be tried with fire, might be
found unto praise and honour and glory
at the appearing of Jesus Christ."

1 Peter 1:7

Sunshine

The sun will shine on anyone
who'll get out in it.

"Truly the light is sweet,

and a pleasant thing

it is for the eyes to behold the sun."

Ecclesiastes 11:7

## Jesus Our Heart Fixer

God knows how to take any confusion and make sense out of it.

He is a heart fixer and a mind regulator. He is the best way-maker there is. He can make a way for you when no one else can.

"Cause me to know the way wherein
I should walk; for I lift up
my soul unto thee."

Psalm 143:8

## God's Timing

God's timing is perfect. God is not our flunky or our busboy. You just can't draw up your own blueprints and hand them over to God and say, 'Here, J.C., carry out these blueprints. Follow them explicitly and oh, yes! — hurry-up.' It won't work.

If you ask God for help while you are in a turbulent situation, He will work it out, but in His time and in His way. Let go of it and let God handle it. We have to turn it loose and allow Him to move His way. He can work it out for your good regardless of the situation or circumstances.

"To every thing there is a season, and
a time to every purpose under heaven:"

Ecclesiastes 3:1

"He hath made every thing
beautiful in his time:"

Ecclesiastes 3:11

## Don't Depend on People

Don't depend on people. Not even to give you a smile. They may not be able to believe God along with you. They don't have a heaven to put you in or a hell to keep you out of. Pray until you find out what God wants you to do.

"Put not your trust in princes...

in whom there is no help."

Psalm 146:3


"Happy is he that hath the God of Jacob

for his help, whose hope is

in the LORD his God..."

Psalm 146:5

## Your Words

Is it worth saying? If you say it you are responsible for it. There is power in your speech. Your words are very powerful to you and to whoever is listening to them. If it's not worth praying about, it isn't worth talking about.

Watch your ways and words. Ask the Lord to keep the door of your lips.

"The words of a man's mouth
are as deep waters, and the wellspring
of wisdom as a flowing brook."

Proverbs 18:4

"He that getteth wisdom loveth
his own soul: he that keepeth
understanding shall find good."

Proverbs 19:8

"Set a watch, O LORD,
before my mouth; keep the door of my lips."

Psalm 141:3

## Is It Confidential?

If I am told something in confidence, I will keep it to myself. That means I will think along with my audience instead of voicing my opinion. Someone may be depending on me to keep it confidential. There are no casual comments! Everybody has a reason for saying anything.

"(Love) Beareth all things,..."

1 Corinthians 13:7

"...for he knoweth the secrets of the heart."

Psalm 44:21

# Is It God's Will?

You can determine if something is or isn't in God's will by asking:

1) Can you back it up with the Word of God?

2) Does it line up with God's holy Word?

3) Is your conscience clear?

4) Are you being honest?

5) God's will is revealed in His Word. The perfect will of God is not determined by chance.

*"For that ye ought to say,*
*If the Lord will, we shall live,*
*and do this, or that."*

James 4:15

*I*

*am in*

*God's Perfect Place*

*at*

*God's Perfect Time*

*doing*

*God's Perfect Will*

## Trouble

Everything is going to be all right, even though there seems to be complete outer chaos. Trouble won't last always.

Waiting on God (in silent prayer) will still your mind. It will allow all the spiritual dust to settle down. Thinking and worrying won't change you or your situation. When storms in your life are raging all around you and it looks like total disaster, ask God to stand beside you and with you. God's still got it. He never loses it! You can't ever surprise God. He knows all about it. It's going to be all right.

"They soon forgat his works;
they waited not for his counsel."

Psalm 106:13

## *Tough Decisions*

Ask yourself about your motive. Am I doing this for myself, or for the glory of God in my life? Is it to satisfy my own ambition, or is it to further the kingdom of God?

Am I willing to wait on God until He opens the door or am I trying to push my own door open by myself? Doing nothing is sometimes wise.

Sometimes we try to push the door open just in case God doesn't know what He's doing. We get ahead of God. Will I wait for God to arrange the structure of my life? God doesn't have to rush anywhere because He's always on time. An impulsive spirit shows lack of faith. We don't ever have to help God along. He always knows what He's doing. He knows who you are and where you are. He also knows where you need to be. Help is on the way; so, you just rest in the Lord. God's not nervous. He'll take care of it and you. He'll still be God forever.

If you should face an emergency, act intelligently, don't panic.

"God is our refuge and strength,
a very present help in trouble."

Psalm 46:1

# Who Am I, Really?

Be happy to be who you are. There is a tremendous sense of freedom when you just be yourself. There will never be another you. You are you. When you were conceived you were the champion over several million. God chose you. You are you. I know who I am. I am a chosen child of God.

You are here on this earth right now for a purpose, however humble that purpose may be. We responded to His love. God has a plan for your life. You can't pretend. Grow up! Be who you really are.

God will eventually get your attention. God is happy that we belong to Him. He needs us for His own will to be accomplished. He doesn't need us half as much as we need Him. God is tired of Christians playing games. I want the reality of God. I want to be the woman God wants me to be. I want to be the part of the body of the church I was intended to be. We must know who we are in Christ.

We must know what Christ has done for us.God is so personal. God knows all about us and although we all still have weaknesses and failures, He loves us in spite of them all.

"We love him, because

he first loved us."

1 John 4:19

# *Peace*

Even in the church today it's hard to find Christians who have peace and who are resting in God. They're so filled with turmoil and anxiety. We can't expect to find strength in ourselves—we'll fail, that's what we do best.

Look to Jesus. Jesus loves us so much that He died for us. We can trust Him with our lives, our minds and our tomorrows. We need to refuse to monkey around with self. Sheep don't need a psychiatrist. They're not worried. They know the shepherd leads them beside the still waters and green pastures.

We all have moods and down days, not to mention troubles and nagging problems. You can't have God's peace until you allow Him to give you His peace. We can't have His peace of mind if we are fretful, anxious, worried about what someone has said to us or what it looks like.

*"And the peace of God, which passeth
all understanding, shall keep your hearts
and minds through Christ Jesus."*

Philippians 4:7

*"Casting all your care upon him;
for he careth for you."*

1 Peter 5:7

## *Patience*

Read the Bible more and more. Jesus summed it up on the cross when He said, "It is finished." (John 19:30)

He delivered me from myself. He delivered me from my worrying. He defeated all the demons in hell and got it all buried then gave us new life.

A little child has everything he needs to develop, grow and train. He has his DNA and talents. We have everything we need for purification, victory and growth. God is doing a work in us while we are on this earth. He is developing patience within us because there are some things that can't get accomplished in heaven.

Angels even look into us. They consider us a mystery in that they have not experienced this thing called salvation. They are created messengers of God.

Quietly wait in His presence. The assurance that He has it all under control will bring patience into our minds.

"According as his divine power hath given unto
us all things that pertain unto life and godliness,
through the knowledge of him that
hath called us to glory and virtue."

2 Peter 1:3

"...that have preached the gospel unto you
with the Holy Ghost sent down from heaven;
which things the angels desire to look into.
Wherefore gird up the loins of your mind..."

1 Peter 1:12-13

"It is good that a man should both hope and
quietly wait for the salvation of the LORD."

Lamentations 3:26

## *Wisdom and Understanding*

Pray for God's understanding. Jesus is the way. Whatever you need God has it.

It may be a spiritual need such as virtue or something material. Either way, we appropriate it by faith to meet our specific need.

The Bible is the mind of God.

"Trust in the LORD
with all thine heart; and lean not
unto thine own understanding."

Proverbs 3:5

"For the LORD giveth wisdom:
out of his mouth cometh
knowledge and understanding."

Proverbs 2:6

## Change

Life is motion. Life is change. God may be making changes in your life. Pray that you will adjust to these changes. God will always come to you when you need Him, especially when you need Him most. He will make changes for your benefit.

*"...greater is he that is in you,*

*than he that is in the world."*

1 John 4:4

*"But my God shall supply*

*all your need according to his riches*

*in glory by Christ Jesus."*

Philippians 4:19

## My Time

We sell ourselves short when we live for ourselves. If I live several more years, I will be rather old and may not have the strength I now have; so, I will be careful not to waste my time.

*"My times are in thy hand..."*

Psalm 31:15

# I Will Pray for Myself

Friends may love you. They will love you and pray for you; but then go on about their own business. The blind man had to seek Jesus for himself, just like the woman with the twelve-year issue of blood, the leper, Daniel, Jonah and Paul. That is why we need to pray for ourselves. Someone else's prayers may enrich yours, but it's yours that get to the point of your own specific and personal need.

It's your faith that does it. Somebody else's faith is just not the way it's done. It takes God to bear your burdens and solve your problems. We have to go through things for a purpose in our lives. It all depends on how much you are willing to trust and obey God and depend on Him.

Other people are not responsible for you. Nobody can confess your sins for you. We must work out our own soul's salvation. It doesn't matter how much someone else prays for you. It is how much faith you have in God. You must pray for yourself.

When David took Bathsheba he knew it was sin. He knew and God knew.

Your own prayers accomplish the whole purpose—your total purpose for you.

"Against thee, thee only, have I sinned,
and done this evil in thy sight....
Purge me with hyssop, and I shall be clean:
wash me, and I shall be whiter than snow."

Psalm 51:4, 7

"When my spirit was overwhelmed
within me, then thou knewest my path."

Psalm 142:3

## God's Best

God is in control of your life.
Let Him work it out.
Tell Him that you want
His best and only His best—
His very best.

"And we know that all things
work together for good to them
that love God, to them who are
the called according to his purpose."

Romans 8:28

"He that spared not his own Son,
but delivered him up for us all,
how shall he not with him also
freely give us all things?"

Romans 8:32

## Difficult Situations

God is always present. Even when we think God is absent, He is still present. He allows His seeming absence so our deep difficult situations can call to His deep resources. People can pity us, but only God can help us.

Sometimes it takes certain circumstances to encourage us to seek God. He wants us to want Him more than anything else He can give us.

"...he knowth the secrets

of the heart."

Psalm 44:21

## *Forgiveness*

We may need forgiveness for not paying attention to God's leading or for our prayerlessness or for our impatience or critical spirit, or lack of sympathy. He tells us that we are His and that He is taking care of us.

Forgiveness from God removes the burden of sin off of our own life. We all need forgiveness—forgiveness for a critical spirit, prayerlessness, pride, haughty or spiteful spirit, judging people.

But, just because we forgive someone else doesn't mean we need to live with a repeated offense. Tolerance is not forgiveness. People need to decide what they can and cannot live with. Work it out either between both of you or within the group.

"Though I walk in the midst of trouble,
thou wilt revive me: thou shalt stretch
forth thine hand against the wrath
of mine enemies, and thy right hand
shall save me. The LORD will perfect
that which concerneth me: thy mercy,
O, LORD, endureth forever: forsake
not the works of thine own hands."

Psalm 138: 7-8

# Why Am I Here?

At the time of procreation there were over a million living seeds. God chose you for conception, birth and life. He has seen you through up until now and He is able to see you through the rest of the way. It has taken years from birth to become a new creation in Christ Jesus. God is always ready to bring us to higher heights and deeper depths in Him. It is actually us who may not be ready for the next step, not Him. He eventually gets us to where we will call upon His name.

"My substance was not hid from thee,
when I was made in secret, and curiously
wrought in the lowest parts of the earth."

Psalm 139:15

"For we are his workmanship, created
in Christ Jesus unto good works..."

Ephesians 2:10

## An Angel of Light

Everything that looks good to us is not always good for us. The devil was the most beautiful creature in the garden. He also was the most subtle.

The devil will give you something that will break your heart or your back or both. We don't have another lifetime to do it over again. Life is not a dress rehearsal. This is it! I've got to get into the right lane now. I need the right answers and the right faith.

"And no marvel;
for Satan himself
is transformed
into an angel of light."

2 Corinthians 11:14

## Don't Take It Back

Frustration is when you give a problem to God and then take it back. We don't have a right to question God. We must just keep having faith. Keep on praising Him and if it's God's perfect will for your life, He'll give you the desire of your heart every time.

Anything you have ever done or said that makes you feel less than who you really are in Christ Jesus, give it to God. Jesus knows. He is into everything. He bore all of our sins. We pray for others but work on ourselves.

"Delight thyself also in the LORD: and
he shall give thee the desires of thine heart."

Psalm 37:4

## Cast Down Imaginations

We must cast down imaginations. Feelings or emotions are undependable as a point of reference. We just have to wait and depend on the leading of the Holy Ghost. Don't depend on feelings (vain imaginations). Get rid of them quickly. Cast them out of your mind. Think about what God tells you in the Word of God.

The Word of God is dependable.

"Finally, brethren, whatsoever things are true,
whatsoever things are honest, whatsoever things
are just, whatsoever things are pure, whatsoever
things are lovely, whatsoever things are of good
report; if there be any virtue, and if there
be any praise, think on these things."

Philippians 4:8

"Casting down imaginations, and every
high thing that exalteth itself against the
knowledge of God, and bringing into captivity
every thought to the obedience of Christ;"

2 Corinthians 10:5

## A Merry Heart

Don't grieve your own spirit. Think on good. A merry heart has the same effect as a medication. A sad and broken spirit dries the bones and joints into osteoporosis and arthritis.

Just because you're in a storm, don't give up! Hold on to God. He will not let you crash all the way. If you're at the boiling point, ready to explode, sing anyway. Don't accept defeat. The enemy comes to steal your joy. The devil doesn't care. God does. Hum a tune. Express your love to the Lord. Tell Him how much He really means to you and how grateful you are for His tender care and direction in your life. If you are trusting God you can sing.

Don't let the devil press you down. God rides on wings of mercy and love. Ride with Him. Every day I will humble myself before God and declare Psalm 118:24.

Start every day fresh and new. A good bubble bath may help you to relax. Try to get a good night's rest every night, too. Sing and get happy. Wash the dishes with a song. Jesus dwells in the praises of His people. Singing a happy song is the start of welcoming in the presence of God.

God is continually maturing us.

Watch your ways and words. Ask the Lord to keep the door of your lips.

Ask Him to place a group of holy angels around you and keep you under the blood. We need Jesus for our shield of protection.

God may use people to give you a word in due season, a word of wisdom and or direction. If it is a true word from God, it will always agree with the written Word of God.

"Beloved, think it not strange concerning the
fiery trial which is to try you, as though some
strange thing happened unto you: But rejoice..."

1 Peter 4:12-13

"When I was a child, I spake as a child,
I understood as a child, I thought
as a child: but when I became a man,
I put away childish things."

1 Corinthians 13:11

"And we know that all things work together
for good to them that love God..."

Romans 8:28

"Set a watch, O LORD, before my mouth;
keep the door of my lips."

Psalm 141:3

## Control of My Castle

If you let Him, Jesus will walk down into the courtyard of your life. Then He will come in and compassionately gain control of your castle. He wants to be King of your castle.

We must die to self. I must relinquish control of my castle. There are two roads. One is where we are king and we are running the show. The other is where Jesus is in charge. The road most traveled is the one in the middle that connects the two. We fight for control. Open the iron door so Christ can come in and be in charge of your life. Who is king of your life?

When Jesus comes into your life, He begins His spiritual construction. He tears down and He builds up. He takes control of your heart and the worry and agonizing confusion begins to lift. He fulfills your life. Contentment in Jesus is sweet. Without Jesus in control, your life is the start of all kinds of anxiety and frustration.

Our own desires need to be placed on the altar just like Abraham had to place Isaac on the altar.

"The name of the LORD is
a strong tower: the righteous
runneth into it, and is safe."

Proverbs 18:10

"We love him,
because he first loved us."

1 John 4:19

## Goals In Life

If we don't have goals in life, we get stuck and stagnant. Get constructive and find a way to help somebody. Be a friend to somebody. Love gets what love gives. We reap what we sow. It will help you feel needed in this world. Wait on the Lord in prayer. He will then tell you about you. God changes people. Prayer changes things.

"For I know the plans I have for you,
says the Lord. They are plans for good
and not for evil, to give you a future and
a hope. In those days, when you pray
I will listen. You will find me when you
seek me, if you look for me in earnest."

Jeremiah 29:11-12 TLB

# We Reap What We Sow

We reap what we sow and what we say. God will forgive us for evil words carelessly spoken or a deed carelessly done; but still the seed has been sown and we will reap. We just can't judge people. We must leave that up to God to do later.

David repented in sackcloth and ashes when he committed adultery and murder. Then God gave him a clean heart. You just can't deliberately do wrong and say, 'God, forgive me, I didn't mean it.' It doesn't work that way. You just can't treat people any way you want and expect to please God.

You will reap whatever you sow. Jesus didn't say for us to be his spokesman or puppet. He said to love one another.

"*Be not deceived;*
*God is not mocked:*
*for whatsoever a man soweth,*
*that shall he also reap.*"

Galations 6:7

"*...love one another....*"

John 13:34

## Life

Life is not a fairy tale or a joke. We have one shot at it. Just one. Whatever you decide to do in life, give it your best shot. Ask God to direct you and guide you in every decision you make. If you feel you stepped off the track He can put you back on.

Anything less than God will let you down.

"The law of his God is in his heart;
none of his steps shall slide."

Psalm 37:31

"Let us hear the conclusion of the whole matter:
Fear God, and keep his commandments:
for this is the whole duty of man."

Ecclesiastes 12:13

## If We Won't Listen

If we won't listen to God we will slip and slide and won't get anywhere. I don't want to lean on my own understanding. We need to know God—know His voice.

I want to know His soft gentle voice. I am His. I am in His sheepfold. I ask God for wisdom and understanding.

Wisdom and understanding are more valuable than diamonds, rubies and pearls. God opens our spirit to making right choices and taking the right road. Anything else is a waste of time—our time. Our time on this earth is brief. God is eternal.

"My sheep hear my voice."

John 10:27

"...for the price of wisdom is above rubies."

Job 28:18

"With him is wisdom and strength,
he hath counsel and understanding."

Job 12:13

## The Anointing

If you won't do what He wants you to do, He will anoint someone else to do it. But, it won't be the same as if you did it. He gave you the anointing for that specific project. When God speaks to you to do that something, He wants you to do it and do it His way and on time. Any procrastination is disobedience.

Tomorrow is not promised. Forget the things behind you and press forward. He already knows what is going to happen at any point in time, whether it is one second or ten thousand years from now. That is the reason why you must stay close to His heart and make sure it is the Lord giving you instruction and direction in your life.

"*And it shall come to pass in that day,*

*that his burden shall be taken away*

*from off thy shoulder, and*

*his yoke from off thy neck,*

*and the yoke shall be destroyed*

*because of the anointing.*"

Isaiah 10:27

## Making Right Choices

We buy trouble for ourselves when we make wrong choices. Satan couldn't get us off the right road if we were making right choices. Every moment we are with one spirit or the other. Every moment we are controlled by one of two spirits. Either we are controlled by the Holy Spirit or the spirit of the enemy. Choosing to go with God—that is the right choice. Choosing to go with God and a little bit of Satan, that's a bad combination. That's a bad path.

"Teach me thy way, O LORD,

and lead me in a plain path..."

Psalm 27:11

"...I have set before you life and death,

blessing and cursing: therefore choose life,

that both thou and thy seed may live:..."

Deuteronomy 30:19

## God's Green Light

It's better to stay a little bit behind God than to go ahead of Him. The devil says to do it and do it right now. He stomps his foot and says to do it now, right now. If we do something compulsively we may be deceived into stepping off into big trouble. We need to be sure it is God who is speaking. If we harden our heart and insist on doing it our own little way, we eventually will not be able to hear from God—His own gentle nudging.

When you are seriously determined to wait until God gives you His 'green light' you will have proceeded in the right direction. I will take time to be still and just rest and wait for God's timing. He will let me know when His timing is right.

"Be still, and know that I am God..."

Psalm 46:10

"They soon forgat his works;

they waited not for his counsel."

Psalm 106:13

## *Jealousy*

Jealousy (envy) is a total waste of time. There will always be people who have more and less than you do. Aspire to achieve what you want in life. Don't allow someone else to make you feel like you're not as good as they are because you don't have what they have. God has a unique plan for your life just as He has a plan for theirs.

We need to remember where God brought us from and how much we owe to God. Jealousy rots our bones.

"A sound heart is the life of the flesh:

but envy the rottenness of the bones."

Proverbs 14:30

# Gratefulness

God loves gratefulness.
Gratitude is a beautiful virtue.
It opens the door for God
to give you more.
Gratitude is a virtue
similar to that of humility.

"*Offer unto God thanksgiving;*
*and pay thy vows unto the most High:*
*And call upon me in the day of trouble:*
*I will deliver thee, and*
*thou shalt glorify me.*"

Psalm 50:14-15

# Keep Your Eyes on Jesus

Anyone could wake-up one morning, come into the office and take a dislike to you. They may not like the way you smile or the way you sit down. As long as you keep your eyes on Jesus you'll be all right.

I can encourage myself in the Lord. I know He will be my portion in the land of the living.

God expects us to do what we know. He said if you fall He will pick you up.

He bears you up on wings of mercy. He said He would never leave us.

"For a just man falleth seven times,
and riseth up again: but the wicked
shall fall into mischief."

Proverbs 24:16

"...for he hath said, I will never
leave thee, nor forsake thee."

Hebrews 13:5

## Discouragement

When you get discouraged, pray and reach out to God. Praise is the bridge that carries you over. You just praise God, regardless of what goes up or comes down. Keep God first. Let God know that your life is still in His hands. Keep your eyes on Jesus and have faith in God.

The reason we have so many suicides is that people don't know how to reach out to God. They just don't know how. Human thinking and human nature (flesh) is our enemy because Satan can control it. People are walking around in a dead stupor or dead attitude because the Lord is not in their thoughts. Our flesh can get us into trouble when we think thoughts not orchestrated by God and His Holy Spirit.

The devil tried to fight against Gabriel, the archangel of God, from bringing Daniel the answer; but all he could do was to delay God's message.

God is willing to give us whatever we need when we ask Him and believe Him to do it.

"Then said he unto me, Fear not, Daniel:

for from the first day that thou didst set

thine heart to understand, and to chasten

thyself before God, thy words were heard,

and I am come for thy words....

But the prince of the kingdom of Persia

withstood me one and twenty days..."

Daniel 10:12-13

## Let God Do It

God will be with you as long as you let Him and believe Him. Hold on to God regardless of what it looks like on the surface. Let Him be with you. If you find yourself in a difficult situation hold your tongue, your tears, your efforts and let the Lord fight your battle.

Hold on to God's unchangeable hand.

"...Be not afraid nor dismayed
by reason of this great multitude;
for the battle is not yours, but God's."

2 Chronicles 20:15

## God Doesn't Mock Us

God can bless you any way He wants to. He will lift you up, not put you down. God doesn't mock us. He doesn't give us something then take it away. He doesn't work that way.

Get quiet and alone with God and find out what He wants you to do. Get real with Him and yourself. You can't fool God. You can only fool yourself. Get at peace with God and you. Get happy and stay secure in the Lord Jesus.

*The blessing of the LORD,*

*it maketh rich, and he addeth*

*no sorrow with it."*

Proverbs 10:22

# God's Viewpoint

God can use you any way He wants to. We need to place our trust in God regardless of what the devil does or tries to do to us. God didn't bring us this far to desert us.

See the situation from God's viewpoint. Don't let the devil press you down. You don't have anywhere to go anyway; so just trust God to work it out. You only have God to turn to. He's all you have. He is the only one who can help. People can pity us but only God can help us. God will open your eyes to things. God changes people through prayer.

*"Open thou mine eyes, that*
*I may behold wondrous things..."*

Psalm 119:18

## The Victory

We supply the will and God supplies the power. We only get the victory when we are willing to fight for it. We have to want the victory; then He gives us the power through the Holy Spirit. Go to church and work out your own salvation. The preacher can't work out your salvation, neither can your friends — some of them you may outgrow. Get serious with God.

I want to do it His way. We think that our way is best when actually we don't have a way. I don't have a way. I want Him to have full control in my life. We can't play games with God. He doesn't play our little games. God is already into the future. Go with Him who knows the future and has all knowledge and wisdom. He is wiser than wisdom. He created wisdom. We must continually change to become more like Him. He is the same yesterday, today and forever.

"But thanks be to God,
which giveth us the victory
through our Lord Jesus Christ."

1 Corinthians 15:57

## Fiery Darts

Don't let every little dart (cutting word or comment) and every little snare, or wrong attitude that the wicked set before you sting you, hurt you and give you anxiety or stress or high blood pressure or frustrate you.

Let the peace of God rule in your heart and mind. If your boss comes in some morning and doesn't smile, it may be that his wife burnt the toast. She may have used his favorite old toothbrush to polish the silver the night before.

We can't let peace rule when we are full of fear and anxiety. We can't stay so preoccupied with them and always hot under the collar about what somebody said or what we think about it that the peace can't stay. These are the little foxes that Solomon spoke about when he said they spoil the vines.

We can't let peace reign when our heart is pounding. Where is the relaxation, the serenity? Keep those darts and snares out of your spirit. Lift high your shield. Toughen up your spirit "skin" with the Word of God.

Let the peace of God rule in your mind.

"Great peace have they which love thy law:
and nothing shall offend them."

Psalm 119:165

"Thou wilt keep him in perfect peace, whose mind
is stayed on thee: because he trusteth in thee."

Isaiah 26:3

"Above all, taking the shield of faith,
wherewith ye shall be able to quench
all the fiery darts of the wicked."

Ephesians 6:16

"And the peace of God, which passeth
all understanding, shall keep your hearts
and minds through Christ Jesus."

Philippians 4:7

"...the foxes, the little foxes, that spoil the vines:
for our vines have tender grapes."

Solomon's Song 2:15

## Lonely or Alone

Never confuse loneliness with being alone. A person can be lonely in a crowd of people. When we are aware of the Holy Spirit around us, we are not lonely. Pray continually and stay close to the Lord. He will guide, guard, direct and protect you. He promised that He would never leave us, never.

*"When my father and*
*my mother forsake me,*
*then the LORD will take me up."*

Psalm 27:10

*"...for he hath said, I will never*
*leave thee, nor forsake thee."*

Hebrews 13:5

# Insults

Don't let every little word or insult bend you out of shape. When someone shoots a fiery dart of insult at you, you don't have to accept it. You can change your attitude from self-pity to that of assuming your shield of faith.

People may say anything, but never allow their slander to wound you. Keep that shield of faith ready to protect your emotions. It is impossible to stay in peace when we are in turmoil and our feelings are in question. Don't let someone else's attitude determine your attitude. Tell Jesus. Tell him all about it. You can't handle your emotions anyhow, but He can.

If you're worried that someone is going to belittle you or go too far with you, give your pride to God. He's not going to belittle you or hurt you or scorn you or make fun of you or mess you around. Don't allow the people pleasing spirit. Jesus will exalt you above every problem and keep you safe from anything the devil can do to you.

If someone reflects a spirit of malice or jealousy, let them do that for themselves, but don't confess, 'I won't let anyone get away with that. You just can't do that to me. It's against my principles.' Don't ponder on it. Don't worry about things. Trust God just for today. Don't keep in your mind what you don't want there. Don't remember it. Dismiss it right away. Cast it down and away from your mind. Release it.

"Casting down imaginations,
and every high thing that exalteth
itself against the knowledge of God,
and bringing into captivity every
thought to the obedience of Christ."

2 Corinthians 10:5

## The Future

The best is yet to be. Only God knows what is in your future. Unless He reveals something to you, you cannot know what lies ahead. We just need to trust and obey God. These two things are very important to our present and future.

God has your each and every day planned in advance. He wrote the book about your life even before you were born. That is just how much He loves you.

"Thine eyes did see my substance, yet being
unperfect; and in thy book all my members were
written, which in continuance were fashioned,
when as yet there was none of them."

Psalm 139:16

"He hath showed thee, O man, what is good;
and what doth the LORD require of thee,
but to do justly, and to love mercy,
and to walk humbly with thy God?"

Micah 6:8

## Obedience

Be permanently convinced that you are going to operate in faithful obedience to God. In all that you do in life, stay

Poised    Patient    Positive

Keep a smile on your face. It's a lot easier to keep company with someone who is cheerful. Stand firm. Stand still. Keep your equilibrium. Keep your balance.

Obedience is better than anything you can give God. When God points you into a certain direction, He expects you to walk in it.

Submitting to the Lord's way is far less complicated than struggling to get your own little way. Keep on praising Him. Pray in the Spirit. You don't know what to pray, but God does. The Holy Spirit does. Faith rests. It doesn't struggle. Cast your burden upon the Lord. God made us in His image, the Father, the Son, and the Holy Ghost.

*"And Samuel said,*
*Hath the LORD as*
*great delight in burnt offerings*
*and sacrifices, as in obeying*
*the voice of the LORD?*
*Behold, to obey is better*
*than sacrifice, and to hearken*
*than the fat of rams."*

1 Samuel 15:22

## The Cherry and the Pit

Learn what you can from all your teachers whomever they are. If there is any good in their lessons, eat the cherry but spit the pit! Remember the best and forget the rest.

"Those things, which ye have
both learned, and received,
and heard, and seen in me, do:
and the God of peace
shall be with you."

Philippians 4:9

## Salvation

"If we confess our sins, he is faithful
and just to forgive us our sins, and
to cleanse us from all unrighteousness."

1 John 1:9

"For with the heart man believeth unto
righteousness; and with the mouth
confession is made unto salvation."

Romans 10:10